Treasures Forever

ROCKPORT

Treasures Forever

Connie Sheerin and Janet Pensiero

ROCKPORT PUBLISHERS

CRAFTS FOR KEEPING FAMILY MEMORIES

First published in the United States of America by
Rockport Publishers, Inc.
33 Commercial Street
Gloucester, Massachusetts 01930-5089
Telephone: (978) 282-9590
Fax: (978) 283-2742
www.rockpub.com

Library of Congress Cataloging-in-Publication Data
Sheerin, Connie.
    Treasures forever : crafts for keeping family memories / Connie
Sheerin and Janet Pensiero.
        p.   cm.
    ISBN 1-56496-848-0 (paperback)
    1. Handicraft. 2. Souvenirs (Keepsakes) 3. Photographs—
Conservation and restoration. 4. Gifts. I. Pensiero, Janet. II. Title.
TT857 .S53 2002
745.593—dc21   2001007511

ISBN 1-56496-848-0

10 9 8 7 6 5 4 3 2 1

Photography: Bobbie Bush Photography
Design and Production: *tabula rasa* graphic design
Copy editor: Pamela Hunt
Proofreader: Stacey Ann Follin
Patterns: Roberta Frauwirth

Printed in China

Contents

Introduction

Memories are certainly one of a kind, but at the same time, they are similar for each and every one of us. They begin with the moment we arrive in this world and continue throughout our lifetime. Each day holds a souvenir for us to take to the next day, next decade, or next lifetime. As time travels on, memories become even more precious as we collect the treasures associated with these moments. Some of my fondest memories were etched in mere moments, but they remain a part of who I am for a lifetime. The bond we all share with our treasures and memories creates many friendships that grow even stronger as we bring these artifacts of our lives together in a creative manner to display, share, and enjoy.

Now in my Goddess Years (as I choose to call my current stage of life), I have grown to understand why I have schlepped so many of these little treasures from home to home, with each and every move. Every time I unpack them, another memory is relived. It seemed to me that it was time to assemble these things in some order—creatively is my favorite way.

These thoughts and remembrances are all marvelous and become the real ties that bind us to our family and friends. Even strangers, who may never have known us, gain a clue about our lives and may find inspiration to create new memory pieces. Whose hand will run over the work I have done and wonder what was going through my head while creating this piece? Whose lives will be touched in the future by these things I have created? I think of that often and smile at the thought that one day they will be artifacts for them to ponder.

Through the years, these treasures capture our "firsts," such as something as small as the first curl cut from a baby's head or a fond memory of a day at the beach. Everything that we do is special to us, unique to us, even the smallest event. These memories make up a map that helps another person understand our time, our journey, our contributions during our time here. These memories certainly help us become more aware of how much the important moments really stay with us, although celebrating or remembering these moments changes with the advance of technology. Remember that you are never alone when you have a memory that is treasured forever—all you have to do is look at it and just remember.

Always creating something,
Connie Sheerin

*I*n my opinion, the perfect display for the ultimate trip souvenir is in the National Cathedral in Washington, D.C. One of the stained-glass windows there was designed to commemorate the flight and moon landing of Apollo XI, and embedded in the window is a piece of moon rock. Most of us don't have such spectacular objects to display, nor can we display them in such a grand scale, but the things we collect and treasure are no less precious to us.

Also in Washington are the museums of the Smithsonian Institution—renowned for collections that chronicle the art and history of civilization. These famous collections are awe-inspiring testaments to the people and events that have shaped us. But often it's the efforts of everyday people—in the form of letters, photographs, and legal documents—that give us the most memorable glimpses into the real lives of the people who came before us.

I had to laugh when I saw the ship manifest from 1903 in the Ellis Island Archives that listed my grandfather, age 15, as a barber. Since I knew him at the end of his life as a retired foundry worker, I have to guess that that was the occupation he aspired to as a teenager, alone in a new country, starting out on the journey of his life. Or maybe he was just trying to impress the immigration officials.

Our hope in putting these projects together was that they would inspire families to gather their stories and document them. Use these projects as a jumping-off point for your own family chronicles. At the next family gathering, hand out blank sheets of paper. Have the young ones draw pictures and the older folks write a remembrance. Gather them up and date them. Then pick a medium—decoupage, papier-mâché, bookmaking, sewing—and create a keepsake with them. I guarantee that will be a day no one will forget.

Janet Pensiero

Basics

YOU WILL USE many different techniques to make the projects in this

book. The basic materials you should have on hand to create these

projects are listed in this chapter, along with general information on a

wide variety of craft techniques.

Basic Tools

Having the right tool allows you to make a project with ease. For the projects in this book, you'll need the basics—pencils, erasers, scissors, and masking tape—as well as some specialized items:

A **ruler** and a **grid-lined cutting mat** help you make straight cuts and square corners with little effort.

A good 7" (18 cm) or 8" (20 cm) pair of **straight scissors** is indispensable for crafting. Decorative scissors are also very popular and are great for putting fancy edges on photocopies and photos.

You'll need a **mat knife** to cut mat board or heavy-weight cardboard.

Use a **craft knife** instead of scissors when you need to cut precise measurements. The blades are replaceable, and there are many different sizes and styles available. Always be sure to use a sharp blade.

Needle-nose pliers and **wire cutters** are essential for wire crafting. Use the pliers to make smooth curls and loops. The pliers are also very helpful for holding small items securely when positioning them.

Washable fabric-marking pens are very handy for transferring patterns to fabric. Disappearing ink pens are also available—the marks usually fade after a day or two, but always test the pens on a scrap piece of fabric first.

Permanent fabric markers are available in an array of colors and are perfect for transferring lettering to fabric. You must set most of them with an iron for them to be permanent.

A **hot-glue gun** is great for attaching odd-shaped items to flat or curved surfaces. The glue sets quickly as it cools. Be sure to read the directions for the glue thoroughly before you use it—the temperature to which you need to heat the glue varies from brand to brand, and for the materials you are gluing.

Double-sided adhesive sheets are used for bonding large, flat pieces of paper or cardboard together. The sheets are thin and have a waxed paper carrier sheet on either side to protect the adhesive. Pull one carrier sheet off, and press the adhesive sheet in place. Then remove the other waxed sheet to finish the bond. For smaller areas, use double-sided clear tape.

Spray adhesive can be used on just about any surface for a stain-free, smooth, even layer of glue. Spray adhesive dries quickly, but you can still reposition items after it has dried.

PVA (polyvinyl acetate) is an excellent all-purpose, acid-free adhesive that you can use for most projects. Also known as white glue, it is a quick-drying, plastic-based adhesive that keeps paper flat and dries clear. When diluted, it can also be used for sealing porous surfaces. Apply the glue with a brush, brushing it from the center out to ensure all areas are covered.

Acrylic matte medium is opaque when wet and translucent when dry. It can be used for collages and also works well in adhering paper to glass. It produces a matte, nonreflective finish.

Permanent, quick-grab glue, such as Fabri-Tac and E-6000, is absolutely essential. There's nothing worse than waiting for glue to dry or watching objects slip and slide because the glue hasn't firmed up yet. Quick-grab glues are usually formulated for a variety of surfaces and can be used on almost anything.

Liquid Laminate is an all-in-one laminating product that acts as both the adhesive and the protective covering, and it dries crystal clear. Be sure to test it with each material you are going to use, however, so you can avoid any bleeding of color or writing. Liquid Laminate is great for decoupage. It also bonds, coats, and seals fabrics and papers onto glass, plastic, wood, cardboard, and more.

Archival glue is acid-free and nonstaining, which is important for ensuring your projects are preserved for generations. Archival glue works well with photocopies, photographs, paper, and paper trims for all of your memory work and crafting, collages, and even glitter writing. It is fast-setting and dries clear, without wrinkling or curling your paper or photos.

Epoxy glues—such as Glass, Metal & More—are clear-drying, all-purpose glues that you can use with several materials. Make sure your surfaces are clean and dry, and be sure to protect your work area. Test the glue on a scrap area first, and then apply it evenly with light pressure. This glue sets in about 30 minutes and fully cures in 24 hours.

Several of the projects are made with **handmade paper,** which can be found at craft and rubber-stamp stores, by mail order, and on the Internet. You can also find unique papers for computer printers at office supply stores in a range of colors and textures. Both handmade and computer paper work great for the pages of handmade books and as accents in decoupage projects. Tracing paper is useful for copying artwork and transferring lettering.

Rubber stamps offer an assortment of ready-made artwork for crafters. You can also find alphabet stamps, which are handy for telling stories, in many styles and sizes. You can press the stamps into polymer clay for a 3-D effect or into embossing ink and powder to create the effect of raised engraved type. Sprinkle the powder over the stamped image, and shake off the excess. Then heat the image with a heat gun (specially designed for this use) to achieve a raised, glossy image.

A few good **brushes** are all you'll need to do these projects—a 1½" (4 cm) flat brush to paint large areas, a #8 or #6 round brush for any detail work, and several foam brushes for the acrylic sealer and decoupage finish. Brushes designed for special purposes, like stenciling, are also available. Remember, you'll get the best results using a high-quality brush.

A few other tools you might want to have ready include a screwdriver, tweezers, cotton swabs, rubbing alcohol (for cleaning your brushes), newspapers (to cover work surfaces while painting), clear adhesive tape, and straight pins.

Basic Techniques

Cutting Paper Products with a Knife

Always use a sharp blade and work on a cutting mat. Cutting mats are useful because they help you align and measure your pieces and protect your work surface. Hold the paper down firmly with a straightedge, and cut along the straightedge with the blade. Keep your fingers away from the path of the blade to avoid any accidents. Don't remove the straightedge before checking that you have completely cut through the paper—you may need to run the blade through twice.

Decoupaging

Decoupage is a Victorian art that continues to find easier ways to keep itself current and less time-consuming. Having a good pair of decoupage scissors is very important. The real trick to cutting is to guide the paper into the scissors rather than to force the scissors into the paper. Wonderful prints of every description and theme are available. Wrapping paper offers some great designs—keep your eyes open!

Decoupage medium is a water-based glue, sealer, and finish that can be used for applying paper to all surfaces. It can be applied with a brush or a sponge, and once it dries, it provides a strong, fast-drying, permanent surface. Decoupage medium is available in a variety of finishes, from matte to satin to gloss. You can even find decoupage medium with a slight sparkle that you can use to add a little pizzazz to your piece.

Using Polymer Clay

Polymer clay is a manmade material. It is much more user-friendly and versatile for the home crafter than ceramic clays. To cure polymer clay, bake it in a convection oven, toaster oven, or your own home oven at temperatures ranging from 265° to 275° F (130° C). Read the directions that come with the clay to determine the actual temperature and curing time.

Before using the clay, you must first condition it. You can do this either by kneading it and warming it in your hands, or by rolling it through a pasta machine. Simply fold and roll the clay through the machine until it is soft and pliable. As a general rule, tools that are used for polymer clay should be dedicated to clay and not used in food preparation.

Using Finishes

Add a coat of protective finish to projects that will receive wear and tear, such as furniture or other functional pieces. The finish will protect and waterproof the surface of your project. Apply the finish with a sponge or bristle brush, taking care to follow the specific manufacturer's instructions. Multiple coats are usually recommended for the best protection.

Acrylic varnish is a water-based finish, which can be used to coat and protect any paper project. It is available in matte and satin varieties. It dries quickly, before dust and particles can settle in it, so it is usually not necessary to sand between coats.

Polyurethane is a durable polymer-based finish. Use paint thinner or mineral spirits for cleanup. Polyurethane dries more slowly than acrylic varnish, so you will need to lightly sand your project between coats to smooth out any dust that adheres to the finish.

Making Papier-Mâché

You can either purchase papier-mâché paste in a craft store or make it from scratch by using the recipe for basic flour paste in the book (see page 34). If you store the paste in an airtight container in a cool place, it will keep for several days. Wheat paste, which is used for hanging wallpaper, also works well. Papier-mâché is an easy technique, but remember to allow for drying time between making the layers. Because it can be a messy process, cover your work area with newspapers to keep it clean.

Lettering

If you have beautiful handwriting, by all means use it on your projects. If not, you can print out your text in a variety of typefaces and almost any size from your home computer. To transfer your lettering to a transparent surface, like glass, slip the printout with the lettering behind the surface and trace it with a pen designed for decorating glass or plastic. Some of these pens need to be heat-set to be permanent. Lettering can be transferred onto fabric by placing the printout behind the fabric and holding the two pieces up to a light source. Then you can easily trace the text. To transfer your lettering to opaque surfaces, rub the back of the paper with the lettering with the point of a graphite pencil (a #2 pencil works well). Place the lettering with the graphite rubbing facing the surface to be lettered, and trace the lettering with a sharp pen or pencil. The lettering can then be painted or filled in with marker.

Sewing

The projects in this book that involve sewing are designed for a beginning sewer on a home sewing machine. In addition to the sewing machine, you'll need large and small hand-sewing needles and thread in the color of your choice. If you can sew on a button, you can do the hand-sewing required to complete these projects.

Stenciling

Ready-made or hand-cut stencils are easy to use and readily available. Choose a stencil brush in a size appropriate for the stencil you're using. Oil-based "dry" stencil paint is designed specifically for stenciling, but you can also use acrylic craft paint. If you use acrylic paint, make sure that your brush is slightly dry.

Painting

Acrylic craft paint is easy to use, it dries quickly, and you can clean up with water. Make sure the surface you're painting is clean and dust-free. Always sand rough wood before painting. It's best to use two or three light coats of paint to cover a surface. Use a water-based polyurethane to seal the paint. If you use an oil-based paint, be sure to let it dry for 24 hours between coats. Seal your painted project with an alkyd-based polyurethane.

Laminating

You can laminate documents and photos with clear self-adhesive laminating sheets that you can find in craft and office supply stores. If you're laminating something precious, make sure the laminating sheets are acid free or archival quality. For a less expensive, nonarchival effect, clear contact paper works well. If you're not sure about using the self-adhesive sheets, copy centers can laminate documents and photos for you.

Transfering Images

Iron-on photo transfer paper designed for a home ink-jet printer is great for transferring photos and artwork onto fabric. You can easily create designs on the computer using a graphics program (you may have one pre-installed on your computer) and print them onto the transfer paper. You can also use existing images— family photographs and original children's art can make your projects truly one-of-a-kind. To get your own images into the computer, photograph them with a digital camera or scan them. If you don't have a camera or a scanner available, take your pictures to a photo developer who can burn your favorite photographs onto a CD. Then you can easily transfer the images onto your computer. You can also work with images received via e-mail or through one of the photo Web sites that allow you store images online.

When your design is complete, run a test print on a piece of regular paper. Sometimes colors or design elements appear differently on paper than they do on the screen. Adjust your image until you get it just the way you want it. Print the image onto the iron-on paper using an ink-jet printer or copier. Follow the instructions on the package for ironing the image onto the fabric.

Find a copy center with a self-serve color photocopying machine. With this machine, you can enlarge, reduce, and adjust the color of the photos and documents you're copying. You can even make a color photo into a black-and-white copy or add color to a plain document. You can also ask the people at the copy center to transfer your image onto iron-on transfer paper.

BABIES CHANGE SO FAST. One day they're tiny infants cooing in a bassinet, and the next thing you know, they're toddling off in search of the remote control. Photos are a great way to document this exciting time, and most families keep busy snapping photos during a baby's first year. Most people choose to display their photographs freely in frames or on the fridge, but there are many ways to

Baby Memories

combine photos into a larger keepsake, such as in the First-Year Memory Frame.

In addition to preserving your memories from this time, we've also come up with some ways to save these earliest stories for the baby to look back at as he or she grows up. For example, the Baby Memories Envelope Book provides a wonderful place to stash handwritten family notes, newspaper clippings, and other memorabilia from that first year that will surely be enjoyed when explored in the years to come.

Baby's Stories

There are two kinds of stories to keep for babies. The first are the stories of the family's accomplishments, disappointments, and personalities that make up the baby's history. Surround your newest family member with photos of family and friends. Have members of your extended family write a story or wish, and bind them in a book or collect them in a box. Videotape or record the voices of special people for the little one to listen to and watch as he or she gets older. Write family quotes on fabric with textile markers and sew the fabric into a quilt or wall hanging. Convert some family photos into slides, and hang them from a lamp shade in the baby's room. Create keepsake boxes, which will become treasures to hold all these special things.

The second type of story is unique to the infant—his or her own story in the making. Parents, grandparents, and siblings can all collect and preserve items for the baby's story.

Save newspapers, magazines, and other printed material from the day and month of your child's birth. Pack a small suitcase with items that may be significant as he or she travels through life: the outfit her mother wore to bring her home from the hospital, crepe paper decorations her big brother made to celebrate her christening, pressed flowers from an arrangement at his bris. Growth and change can be fun to document, too. Press a tiny thumbprint into a soft lump of polymer clay, and bake it for a permanent reminder of the tiny hands long after they've grown.

Newborns don't usually have stories to tell, but the family who surrounds the crib listening to their coos and gurgles does. Encourage the members of your extended family—and friends, too—to write a special story or memory for your newest family member. Create this envelope book to hold the reminiscences for the day when your child can read them herself. You can also send the envelopes with blank paper and a request for a story to all your family members. Bind the envelopes—stamps, postmarks, and all—into a book. This book is made out of small square envelopes, but you can use any size you like. See page 98 for a variation of this project.

Baby Memories Envelope Book

MATERIALS

- pastel vellum paper
- square envelope templates
- Rollabind hand punch and binding rings
- ribbon
- clear plastic file folder (available at office supply stores)
- double-sided tape (clear)
- hole punch
- small piece of cardstock
- small sheet of coordinating solid paper
- rubber stamp, embossing ink, and silver embossing powder
- silver metallic marker
- diaper pin (optional)

1. Using a 5" (13 cm)-square envelope template, make approximately eight envelopes using the pastel vellum.

2. Cut a 5¼" x 5⅜" (13 cm x 14 cm) piece of the plastic file folder for the cover. Cut a piece of cardstock the same size for the back cover.

3. Center the hand punch on the side edge of each envelope, and punch holes for the binding rings. Repeat with the front and back covers. Line up the holes, and insert the rings to bind the envelopes between the covers.

4. Create a 2" (5 cm)-square envelope out of a coordinating solid paper using an envelope template. Punch two holes in the center of the envelope, and insert ribbon ends from front to back, and then forward through the holes to end in the front. Using a rubber stamp, embossing ink, and silver embossing powder, create the raised baby pin art. Write your baby's name on the envelope.

5. Tape the small envelope in the center of the front cover using clear double-sided tape.

6. Stamp the baby pin with white ink on a piece of vellum the same size as the cover, to create an all-over effect. Insert the stamped vellum sheet directly underneath the clear plastic front cover.

7. Add a ribbon and a diaper pin to the disks by first drilling a hole in one ring with a small hand drill, and then threading the ribbon through the hole.

Keepsake Tip

Family members can write special stories and insert them in their own envelopes. Envelopes can be added or removed at any time.

family stories for Katie

Design: Janet Pensiero

I knew from the minute that I saw my first great nephew, Chase, that the camera loved his face. I created this project for his mother, Amanda, to document his first year, because babies change and grow so much during that time. You can adapt this idea for just about any subject—the first year of school, a sports season, or a memorable vacation or trip. You can be sure that it will be cherished forever.

First-Year Memory Frame

MATERIALS

- picture frame, for an 8" x 10" (20 cm x 25 cm) picture with 3" (8 cm) width
- spray paint (color of your choice)
- 12 glass squares, 2" x 2" x ⅛" (51 mm x 51 mm x 3 mm)
- one package of dried flowers and greenery
- self-adhesive silver foil tape, ¼" (6 mm) width
- 12 color photocopies to be cut to 2" x 2" (5 cm x 5 cm)
- photograph, 8" x 10" (20 cm x 25 cm)
- acid-free glue
- white glue
- scissors
- clear tape
- tweezers
- ballpoint pen

1. Spray-paint the frame, following the directions on the can. Cover the frame thoroughly.

2. Using a glass square as a template, draw a cutting line around each photocopy by tracing around the edge of the glass with a ballpoint pen. Then cut out each picture.

3. Use the tweezers to add the dried flowers and greenery to the corners of each picture with the white glue.

4. Secure each cut-out photocopy to a glass square with a small piece of clear tape on the top and bottom. Once the glass is in place, cut 2" (5 cm) pieces of the silver foil tape. You will need eight pieces of the silver foil tape per picture. Adhere one piece at a time to each side of the front of the picture. Then flip the square over, tape all four sides of the back to the frame, and seal each picture.

5. Carefully spread a thin, even coat of the acid-free glue to the back of each glass square and photocopy piece, and glue the squares over the entire frame.

6. Insert the 8" x 10" (20 cm x 25 cm) photograph in the frame.

Design: Connie Sheerin

I asked my mother to look through her collections to find items to inspire me for this book. Amazingly, she found the first curl that was cut from my locks when I was almost two years old. She had sent the curl to my grandmother, and it had eventually found its way back to my mother. Now that I'm in my "goddess" years, that first curl seems even more important. I especially loved my grandmother's handwritten date on the envelope and my pictures—both before the curl was clipped and after, at my second birthday. Embellish your shadowbox with any special objects, from a favorite toy to a tiny shoe to a baby spoon.

Baby Keepsake Shadow Box

MATERIALS

- color photocopies of baby's memorable events
- small items symbolizing infancy
- textured acid-free background paper
- Plexiglas box frame with a white cardboard box insert
- archival glue
- white craft glue
- one package of dried flowers and greenery
- tweezers
- craft knife
- lace and trim
- double-sided tape
- sawtooth hanger

1. Cut out the front of the cardboard box insert with a craft knife, and use the archival glue to cover the inside of the box with the textured acid-free paper. Make sure to cover up to the edges of the box—you can use lace and trim to hide any rough edges. Be careful not to make the edge too thick because the cardboard insert needs to fix back inside the Plexiglas frame when you are finished.

2. Arrange and glue down all of the pieces you have gathered. Use the archival glue for photocopies and a thick white glue for the small objects.

3. Use the tweezers and the archival glue to attach some dried flowers and greenery for embellishment.

4. Clean the Plexiglas carefully, and slide the cardboard insert back inside the box frame to finish the shadow box.

5. Use double-sided tape or glue to attach a sawtooth hanger so you can hang the box on wall. You can also prop it up on an easel.

Keepsake Tip

These inexpensive box frames are available in many discount and craft stores in a wide selection of sizes. To determine the size of frame that you'll need, lay out all the items and photocopies that you want to include.

Design: Connie Sheerin

Chase Joseph Cole came into this world in September 2000. His mother, my niece Amanda, gave the family the first baby in 22 years—what a joy! A new baby truly warms the heart and brings everyone together to celebrate life. This is a special box for my grandnephew to help his mother begin saving the wonderful things that make memories. This box can be customized to fit just about any special moment in life to hold the trinkets that mean so much as the years go by.

Chase's Memory Box

MATERIALS

- hinged wooden box, 11" x 4" x 3" (28 cm x 11 cm x 8 cm)
- baby-motif floral container
- three bags of ³/₄" (2 cm) tiles (one each of baby blue, white, and yellow)
- mosaic glue
- craft stick
- tile nippers
- baby blue acrylic paint
- black permanent felt-tip marker
- one bag of miniature star and moon decorations
- four white drawer pulls
- one white button
- buttercream sanded grout
- sandpaper
- graphite paper
- clean soft cloth

1. Lightly sand the wooden box, and apply two coats of baby blue acrylic paint, both inside and out.

2. To create the mosaic pattern for the top of the box, first nip the floral container into small pieces to create the main animal images. Arrange these pieces, leaving space between them to fill in with the colored tiles. When you are happy with the design, glue the pieces to the box using mosaic glue.

3. Fill in the spaces with the blue, white, and yellow tiles, nipped into the appropriate size, and secure them with mosaic glue. Finish off the edge of the box by alternating the colored tiles cut to fit around the lid edge.

4. Mix the grout according to the directions on the package until it is a fudge-like consistency. Then add the baby blue paint to the grout, a few drops at a time, and continue to mix it until you get it the shade you desire (the grout will dry a bit lighter). The grout is ready to use when its consistency is firm, but moist. Grout the mosaic, let it dry for 15 minutes, and then wipe with a soft cloth. Wait another 15 minutes, and you will see a haze appear. Clean off the rest of the excess grout, and polish the mosaic with a clean soft cloth. Allow the grout to dry overnight.

5. Make a paper pattern of the side of the box, and hand-letter the child's name on the pattern. Then use the graphite paper to trace your lettering onto the box. Go over the lettering with a black permanent felt-tip marker.

6. Glue the white button to the lid of the box to create a handle. Glue the decorations for embellishment. Glue the four white drawer pulls to the bottom of the box to act as feet.

Keepsake Tip

Check out yard sales and thrift stores for baby-motif floral containers or drawer pulls for the feet. If the drawer pulls aren't the right color, you can always paint over them to coordinate with the broken tiles used on the top.

Design: Connie Sheerin

Everyone has some pictures that they'd like to frame in a special way. A unique and lasting method of displaying a favorite picture is to put it into a paperweight that can be propped up on an easel or just placed on a desk or end table. For a unique twist, try starting with black-and-white pictures, and hand-color them first.

Baby's Paperweight

MATERIALS

- glass tile, 4" x 4" x ¾" (10 cm x 10 cm x 2 cm)
- color photocopies of pictures and smaller head shots
- Liquid Laminate
- rubber gloves
- decoupage scissors
- mat board, cut slightly smaller than the glass tile
- felt for backing or round felt feet
- black, fine-line, permanent, acid-free pen
- damp paper towel
- metal easel (optional)
- archival glue

1. Make color photocopies of your pictures. Then cut and arrange the photocopies on the mat board, working from the background to the foreground.

2. After you have arranged your pictures and trimmed them to fit, glue the design together using the archival glue.

3. Use the black fine-line pen to add any written comments or memories.

4. Put on the rubber gloves and quickly cover your composition and the glass tile with the Liquid Laminate. Lay the glass tile over your composition, and press down, using the damp paper towel to wipe up any excess Liquid Laminate. Force the extra liquid from the center of the glass out to the sides. Wipe the tile clean, and let it dry.

5. After the Liquid Laminate has dried, cover the back of the composition with a piece of felt or add felt feet.

6. You can display this little masterpiece on a metal easel or on your desk.

Design: Connie Sheerin

Every year and for every occasion we buy Pop a couple of ties. And every time he gets dressed up he wears one of the ties that we got him.
Matt Carr

PHOTOGRAPHS, ARTWORK, AND OTHER CHERISHED ITEMS can bring back memories of celebrations, of milestones, and of difficult times—all of which make up the experience of growing up. Turning these items into household keepsakes—such as pillows, bowls, and doorstops—not only gives you time to relish the memories that they help you recall but also gives a whole new life to objects that might

Growing Up

otherwise have been cast away and forgotten. These memories of childhood can spark the fire of youth and vitality in your crafts, which can then be passed to others who share in your treasures.

The Family Home

The projects in this chapter represent the "crevices" in the tree trunk of life—those odd things that you discover as you delve through old boxes, which may seem insignificant but still remind you of deeply rooted experiences. From children's artwork to favorite books, this chapter will certainly remind you of some of those growing-up memories, as well as inspire you to create some very special projects. Adapt the projects so that you can use the unique items found among your own possessions.

The doorstop made of a brick from the house I grew up in is one of my all-time favorite projects. Including the general history of the house in the final project greatly interested my entire family, especially the grandchildren. They are now young adults, and as children they played for many hours in that house, but they never really knew its history. My mother, now in her eighties, is such a great storyteller, and fortunately for me, she was able to straighten out and fill in facts to many family stories for me. Special thanks to our family matriarch! Take the time to discuss your memories with older members of the family to see what unique details they can add—you may discover startling and wonderful details.

Houses are so special, especially when families have spent several decades in them raising more than one generation. Something is always happening in these homes—the first day of school, a prom, a wedding day, and the bringing home of the first grandchild. This special doorstop means a great deal to my family, and it can make a wonderful house-warming gift for anyone of any age. After all, your home is your castle for storing treasured memories. What objects remind you of your first home? Perhaps you have also saved some part of it, or some of the treasures that had a place there. Those objects can help you get started on projects reminiscent of your early years.

The Fischer Family Home
1946-1981

Matt 12

Pop 80

The clothes we wear become a large part of who we are. Some men have a closet full of clothes; others are happy wearing the same T-shirt and jeans over and over. Take that special item and create a keepsake that is certain to generate memories. If your dad or grandfather prefers work shirts or flannel shirts, a patchwork of several patterns would make a lovely pillow cover as well. Sew a pocket from the shirt onto the center of the pillow to hold your written remembrances or even tiny keepsakes. My nephew Matt wrote a story about his Grandpop's ties, and we wrote it onto fabric for the center of this pillow.

Grandfather's Tie Pillow

MATERIALS

- 10 to 12 neckties
- permanent fabric marker
- small scrap of white fabric
- 17" (43 cm) square piece of coordinating fabric for the pillow back
- pattern (see page 105)
- needle and thread
- seam ripper
- scissors
- ruler
- iron
- 16" (41 cm) square pillow form
- cotton fringe trim (optional)
- photo transfer (optional)

1. To prepare the ties, first take them apart with a seam ripper or scissors. Remove and discard the lining and interfacing. Iron the ties to remove the creases. Cut off the point of each tie. Cut each tie to a length of 20" (51 cm), starting at the wide end, and then cut each of these pieces in half lengthwise.

2. Sew the tie pieces together along the long edges in a pleasing arrangement to create a sewn piece approximately 30" x 20" (76 cm x 51 cm).

3. Enlarge the pattern (page 105) on a copy machine so that the long seam line is 16" (41 cm) long. Cut four from the sewn tie piece.

4. Sew along the four angled edges, and iron the seams open.

5. Cut a 4" (10 cm) square of white fabric for the center of the pillow front. Write a message or memory on the square with the permanent fabric marker.

6. Iron the center seams of the tie pieces under, and hand-stitch the white square in place. You can stitch some trim over the seam for a decorative touch.

7. Cut a piece of coordinating fabric 17" x 17" (43 cm x 43 cm) for the pillow back. With the right side of the fabric to the front of the pillow, stitch around three sides of the square. Turn the pillow cover inside out, and insert the pillow form. Hand-stitch the open seam closed. You can sew fringe trim into the outside edge seam if you'd like.

8. If you have a longer story to tell, you can use the entire back of the pillow to write your remembrances. Permanent markers work best on smooth fabric with no nap, like a plain polyester-cotton blend.

Keepsake Tip

Make an iron-on photo transfer at a copy shop or with your computer printer. Iron it onto a small piece of fabric and hand-stitch the fabric to the back of the pillow.

Every year and for every occasion we buy Pop a couple of ties. And every time he gets dressed up he wears one of the ties that we got him.
Matt Carr

Design: Janet Pensiero

Every family has a refrigerator or bulletin board covered with wonderful finger-paint and construction-paper creations made by the children in their lives. The paint that young children use is not permanent and the paper is not very stable, so their artistic treasures don't hold up very well over time. By combining a classic children's craft technique—papier-mâché—and high-tech color copies, you can preserve their masterpieces for years to come, and create a unique decorative bowl that you and your little artist can both be proud of. A paper bowl can be made from color copies of almost anything—photos, postcards, newspaper clippings, first-grade handwriting samples, report cards.

Precious Art Papier-Mâché Bowl

MATERIALS

- color copies of children's art—preferably 11"x 17" (28 cm x 43 cm)
- papier-mâché art paste or homemade flour paste (see recipe below)
- newspaper
- large bowl (such as a smooth plastic salad bowl)
- vegetable oil or petroleum jelly
- one sheet handmade paper (optional)
- water-based polyurethane sealer

Basic Flour Paste

1/2 cup flour
1 teaspoon salt
1 cup warm water

1. Mix the paste to a thick, creamy consistency. It will keep several days if sealed in an airtight container and kept cool. Lightly coat the inside of the bowl with vegetable oil or petroleum jelly so the papier-mâché will be easier to remove.

2. Tear the newspaper into 1 1/2" (4 cm)-wide strips. Dip the strips one at a time into the paste, and remove the excess paste with your fingers. Lay the strips one by one on the inside of the large bowl, slightly overlapping them.

3. After the inside of the bowl is completely covered, let the first layer of paper dry. Once dry, repeat this step 3 or 4 more times to create a sturdy paper bowl. Let dry thoroughly.

4. Carefully remove the paper bowl from the inside of the large bowl.

5. The inside of this paper bowl is lined with some torn pieces of handmade paper. If you like this look, use a torn brown paper bag or any solid-color, colorfast paper.

6. Cut out the copies of the children's artwork, and lay the cutouts inside the bowl in an arrangement that you find pleasing. Glue the cutouts in place using the papier-mâché paste.

7. When the bowl is completely dry, seal it with several coats of water-based polyurethane finish.

Keepsake Tips

- Don't forget to include the artist's name and the date on the bottom of the bowl. (This project features artwork by my niece Katie.)
- You can start small by making smaller bowls using individual salad bowls as your molds.

Design: Janet Pensiero

We know that books have stories to tell. Even children too young to read understand that wonderful stories live on the pages of the books that are read to them by their parents and older siblings. Special books also trigger personal memories and stories—the history of the book itself, happy times spent reading and being read to, or in the case of a cookbook, meals enjoyed. Get the kids involved in creating these hand-me-downs for their younger brothers and sisters by writing their own personal book review. Handmade slipcases inscribed with personal stories will become treasured heirlooms as time passes and the books travel to another generation.

Memory-Wrapped Books

MATERIALS

- favorite books
- acid-free paper or cardstock
- archival glue
- acid-free adhesive mounting sheets
- acid-free pen
- ruler
- scissors
- craft knife
- rubber stamps, acid-free ink, embossing powder (optional)

1. To make the slipcase, first measure the width of the cover and the thickness of the book. Double this measurement and add 2" (5 cm) for the overlap. This measurement is the length of the paper or cardstock that you will use for the slipcase for your book. Determine the height by measuring from the bottom to the top of the front cover.

2. Cut the paper or cardstock to size with the craft knife, and mark off the points on the top and bottom edges where the paper will fold. Connect the points with a pencil, and score the paper along these lines with the dull side of a small scissors. Wrap the cover around the book, and glue the overlap with archival glue.

3. Add pieces of contrasting paper on which you have written your story in acid-free pen or have created some rubber stamp art. If you prefer, you can print the story out using your computer printer and acid-free paper.

4. To make the wraparound cover, measure as above, but fold the ends of the paper around the edges of the front and back covers of the book. Tack the edges of the paper to the inside of the covers with archival glue.

Keepsake Tip

All paper, glue, and ink used on books should be acid-free or pH neutral. Acid-free supplies are readily available in the scrapbook area of craft stores.

Amy Vanderbilt's
COMPLETE
COOKBOOK

LABOULAYE'S
FAIRY
TALES

This book belonged to your
Grandpop when he was a boy.
His parents bought it when
he was a baby. He read it to me
when I was little and your father
and I read it to you. Someday
you'll read it to your children.
Love,
Mom

Design: Janet Pensiero

Built in 1910 by a Mr. Schilling as a custom home for his daughter and her husband, 321 Owen Avenue stood proudly on its half-acre of land for all to admire. My father, F. Theodore Fischer, Jr., was the second owner, purchasing the 17-room house in 1946 for $16,500. The deed included the fact that the cost of wallpapering the three floors in 1910 was $75. It also included the stipulation that no farm animals were to abide within the house. We obeyed the deed! I don't know why, but I kept a brick from that house when we left—and now that simple object has become a fun accessory in our new home. If you're moving from or even remodeling your own home, consider saving some architectural remnant, to turn into a keepsake down the road.

Brick House Doorstop

MATERIALS

- one standard size brick (even better if you can get one from the house)
- white acrylic paint
- paintbrush
- self-adhesive home-themed stickers
- color photocopy of the house (front and back views)
- color photocopies of home-related saying and pictures
- archival glue
- damp paper towels
- scissors
- Liquid Laminate

1. Paint the top and bottom sides (the two largest sides) of the brick with two coats of white acrylic paint. Leave the sides of the brick in their natural state.

2. Trim the color photocopies of the house pictures so that they fit in the center of each painted side of the brick. Attach them to the brick using the archival glue. Pat the photocopies with a damp paper towel to remove any air bubbles and to make sure the glue fills all the nooks and crannies in the brick. Be sure not to rub the picture or the ink from the color photocopy may rub off.

3. Arrange the self-adhesive stickers as a border at the top and bottom of the brick.

Add the little sayings and pictures to enhance the piece.

4. Print a short history of the house, making sure the entire story will fit on the top side of the brick. Then glue it to the top of the brick using the archival glue. Also, print out the family name and address of the house, and glue them to the front of the brick underneath the picture. You can also add the year the house was built.

5. Cover both painted sides of the brick with two coats of Liquid Laminate. Be sure to coat the trim at the top and the bottom, being careful not to get any on the natural brick.

Keepsake Tip

Use the top of your doorstop to include some historical details about your architectural remnant, such as when the house was built, how many families lived there before you, and any interesting stories about the house.

On the road between the houses of friends grass does not grow. ♥

The Fischer Family Homestead
1946-1981

Design: Connie Sheerin

Almost everyone has a junk drawer—that place in your home where the odd bits and pieces of your life end up. With an old desk or end table drawer, either from the trash or from a thrift store, you can create your own homage to "junk." The items in this project don't have to be fancy. In fact, the kids will enjoy gathering up the things that are meaningful to them and helping to arrange them in the drawer. This shrine contains a small sampling of the junk I've accumulated since moving into my house in 1984. I've written the date I moved in with a metallic paint pen on the outside of the drawer.

Junk Drawer Shrine

MATERIALS

- small empty drawer, or unfinished wooden display box
- acrylic paint (optional)
- hot-glue gun and glue sticks
- white glue or decoupage medium
- E-6000 glue or any one-part epoxy
- assorted tchotchkes
- sandpaper (optional)
- paper, such as take-out menus, receipts, old wallpaper, and greeting cards

1. Thoroughly clean your drawer if you got it from the trash or purchased at a thrift store.

2. You can leave the wood unfinished or do more decorative painting, depending on your taste. If you are going to paint the outside of the drawer, lightly sand the unfinished wood before painting it. Then, cover the back surface and sides with paper—take-out menus, receipts, and old wallpaper. You can also use greeting cards, kids' artwork, or appliance warranties.

3. Gather your tchotchkes, and arrange them in the drawer. Glue the items in place using hot glue for most items, white glue for paper, and E-6000 or one-part epoxy for the odd-shaped, hard-to-hold pieces.

4. Try a little ball fringe for the bottom edge, or if you like sparkle, add some sequins or even tiny Christmas lights.

Keepsake Tip

Tchotchke (also spelled chotchke, and pronounced "choch-key") is a Yiddish word meaning something pretty and decorative, but basically useless.

Design: Janet Pensiero

NEARLY EVERYONE HAS A COLLECTION of family photos, either filed in a shoebox or lovingly arranged in a photo album. But what do you do with all of those things that trigger memories and family stories but don't quite fit neatly into a picture frame or a scrapbook?

Use these projects as a guide and a source of inspiration. If you don't have a collection of kitchen tools to display, hang a few of

Family Memories

the screwdrivers and wrenches that your uncle used to tune up his first roadster. Or you can display a few of those hand-woven loop pot holders that your mother painstakingly created when she was a young girl. Whatever objects you choose to preserve and display will surely be cherished for years to come, and more important, their stories won't be forgotten.

Memorabilia & Collections

When gathering memorabilia to save, think about what makes your family special.

What quirks do your family members have? Do they collect anything? What objects remind you of them or trigger family stories? Keeping the stories alive can be as simple as gluing a handwritten note inside a drawer or on the underside of a special piece of furniture explaining how and why it's important to your family history. Or you can be more creative and assemble a collage of objects that are special to a family member, or memorialize a time in your own history with photos and stories. You can turn fabric that has special memories into a pillow, wall hanging, or quilt. Imagine a quilt made of squares of worn denim from all the jeans you've worn over the years—with embroidered dates, even. Or, you can make a baby quilt using squares of fabric from your maternity clothes.

If you are lucky enough to inherit someone else's collection, your only dilemma is how to display it. Painted racks, shelves, and boxes are great for this, but don't forget to include the stories that are attached to the objects. Collections come in many shapes. The collection of empty wine bottles that your grandfather kept in the basement could become a picture of your grandfather in a picture frame beautifully decoupaged with wine labels, recalling his love of good wine.

Sometimes the simplest things remind us of the best stories. If your family spent rainy days in feverish battle over board games that are now too worn and missing too many pieces to use, consider gluing a game board and some piece to a tray or tabletop and sealing it with polyurethane. Every time you use it, it will remind you of the wonderful times you had playing the games together. And remembering is what it's all about.

Travel scrapbooks are great, but they tend to be put away and looked at only on special occasions. Take some of those paper keepsakes that you can't bear to throw away, and preserve them between glass to create functional and memorable coasters. Almost any paper item can be used—photos, ticket stubs, receipts, menus, even foreign money. Tuck a manila envelope or plastic bag in your suitcase to collect the paper memories of your next trip.

Vacation Memory Coasters

MATERIALS

· 4" (10 cm) square plate glass—two pieces for each coaster

· self-adhesive silver foil tape, 1/4" (6 mm) width

· photos, ticket stubs, stationery, and any other paper memorabilia from your trip

· self-adhesive cork squares (optional)

1. Clean and dry the glass.

2. Cut and arrange several pieces of trip memorabilia on a single piece of glass for each coaster. Carefully cut the paper to the edges of the glass. When you have an arrangement you're happy with, place a second piece of glass on top of your arrangement.

3. Hold the two pieces of glass together, with the photos and paper sandwiched in between, and tape around the edge of all four sides with the silver foil tape. If desired, attach the self-adhesive cork squares to the bottom of the coasters.

Keepsake Tip

Make these with your kids using craft foam and self-adhesive cork squares. Laminate copies of photos, and place on the adhesive side of the cork squares. Arrange geometric shapes made from the craft foam around the photos, and fill in the spaces with tiny glass beads.

Design: Janet Pensiero

Every family has its favorite recipe, one that is passed down through the generations, either strictly followed or tweaked just a bit to add new twists. Whether your family's recipe is for apple pie, green bean casserole, or chocolate cookies, you can document it with this easy platter project—a great accessory for any kitchen and fun to pull out for all those family gatherings. My mother made this recipe when we had special company for dinner.

Favorite Family Recipe Platter

MATERIALS

- wooden platter
- polymer clay
- stencil
- acrylic paint
- alphabet stamps
- printed-out or handwritten recipe
- white glue or decoupage medium
- E-6000 glue, any one-part epoxy
- spray acrylic sealer
- craft knife
- gel ink or paint pen
- sandpaper
- damp cloth
- scissors

1. Lightly sand the wooden platter. Wipe with a damp cloth to remove all dust. Apply one coat of paint in the base color of your choice. Let the paint dry, and apply one or two additional coats of paint to completely cover the wood.

2. Print out your favorite recipe from your computer, or hand-write the recipe in a shape to fit the platter. Test the ink with the spray sealer before gluing the recipe in place. Cut out the recipe in an oval shape, and glue it in the center of the platter using the white glue.

3. Roll out a small piece of polymer clay to a thickness of 1/8" (3 mm). Press the alphabet stamps into the clay, and cut the letters into tile shapes with a craft knife. After you've made the alphabet tiles for the name of your recipe, bake them according to the directions for the clay. When the tiles are cool, glue them to the platter with E-6000 glue.

4. Choose a stencil or two, according to the ingredients in your recipe. Stencil the ingredients in the empty spaces on the platter, around the recipe, or on the rim. Add polka dots or other design elements to complement your design.

5. Write a personal memory of the recipe on the platter with a gel ink or paint pen. Seal the entire plate with several light coats of a spray acrylic sealer.

Keepsake Tip

Make color copies of your original recipes, and decoupage the copies to the center of an old china plate or platter with liquid laminate. Cut some colored paper with decorative scissors to use as an accent. Seal the plate with several coats of liquid laminate.

PEARS AU VIN

8 Bartlett pear halves, canned in light syrup
¾ cup red wine
½ cup sugar
½ stick cinnamon

Cook above until sauce thickens. Refrigerate overnight.
Allow 2 halves per serving.
Serve with whipped cream if desired.

for dessert when we had company

Design: Janet Pensiero

As soon as children are old enough to realize that they're part of a family, they start trying to figure out how they fit in. I made this simple four-generation chart to illustrate for my niece and nephew where they came from. To add information and stories, you can pin some badge holders onto the wall hanging with copies of relevant photos—from grandparents' wedding, for example—and documents to illustrate the stories.

Family Tree Wall Hanging

MATERIALS

- 2 yards (1.8 meters) of white polyester-cotton fabric
- acrylic paint, four or five different colors
- leaf shapes (real or fabric leaves)
- black permanent fabric marker
- heavy-weight adhesive plastic laminating film
- grommets
- vintage buttons (optional)
- clear plastic badge holders (optional)
- scissors
- foam brush
- iron
- family tree information, with family lists on separate pieces of paper
- tape
- sewing machine or needle and thread

1. Cut eight pieces of fabric 8" (20 cm) square and three pieces of fabric 10½" (27 cm) square. Trace the leaf shapes, and enlarge them to fit on the individual squares of fabric. When they're large enough, trace the shapes onto the adhesive laminating film, and cut out the leaves. Press the adhesive leaves onto the fabric squares, and paint around the leaf shapes with acrylic paint, using a foam brush. Let them dry, and then iron flat.

2. Gather your family tree information, and lay out each family list on a separate piece of paper. You can hand write the names, or print them from the computer, using a typeface that you like. Place the fabric over the printout, and tape it to a light source, like a light table or a window. Use a permanent fabric marker to trace the names through the fabric.

3. Stitch all the squares together, and join the family members with dotted lines. Sew a border around the edge.

4. Cut a piece of fabric for the back. Place the good side of the fabric against the front side of the wall hanging, and sew around 3 sides. Turn the wall hanging inside out and insert a layer of batting between the front and back. Stitch up the open edge. Hand-tack the layers together at the corner of each square using vintage buttons, if desired.

5. Add grommets to the top and bottom edge to hang.

Keepsake Tips

- Pin on badge holders with photos and documents that help tell the story.
- There are several Web sites that will help you trace your family history. See Resources, on pages 108-109, for details.

Mayer Wasserman
Anna Sobeck
m 1916

John J. Carr
Frances Evans
m 1917

John Jr.
Phyllis
James
Patricia
Paul
Earl
Eunice
Mary Elle

Marie Lorraine
Bernice

m 1943
Jay
Joan
Jeff
Jan
Jar

Design: Janet Pensiero

Family recipes can keep memories of holidays and informal gatherings alive for generations. My Aunt Fran published a cookbook filled with recipes, many going back over 150 years, from family and friends. This cookbook has helped my family retain its Pennsylvania Dutch and German heritage by reminding us how to prepare the dishes our ancestors loved. There is nothing like the aroma of a home-cooked meal to warm the soul and bring back loving memories of family meals and gatherings.

100-Plus Years of Family Recipes

MATERIALS

- metal or wooden recipe box
- miniature rolling pin
- kitchen-themed cutouts and stickers
- utility knife
- Liquid Leaf copper enamel paint
- Liquid Laminate
- archival glue
- hot glue
- recipe cards
- laminator (such as Xyron) (optional)
- small paintbrush
- sponge brush
- color photocopies of your family's "historical" cooks

1. Use the sponge brush to paint the recipe box with two coats of Liquid Leaf Copper Paint, pulling brush lightly over the wood to create the illusion of grain.

2. Arrange the kitchen-theme cutouts and stickers. When you are happy with the design, glue the paper to the box with the archival glue. Make sure you do not leave any air bubbles under the stickers. Allow the glue to dry thoroughly, and then use a utility knife to trim the paper where it hangs over the top and bottom.

3. Write a short history about the family recipes, and print it out on a computer printer. Glue it to the bottom of the box with the archival glue.

4. Apply two coats of Liquid Laminate over all of the paper designs with a small paintbrush, including the history on the bottom of the box.

5. Hot-glue the miniature rolling pin onto the lid of the box to act as a handle.

6. Prepare the recipe cards. You can use one card for each of the family contributors. You can even add a small picture of each contributor on the upper right-hand side of the card, with a short story about that person and their relationship to you. You can laminate the cards to protect them, or not at all—whatever suits your taste.

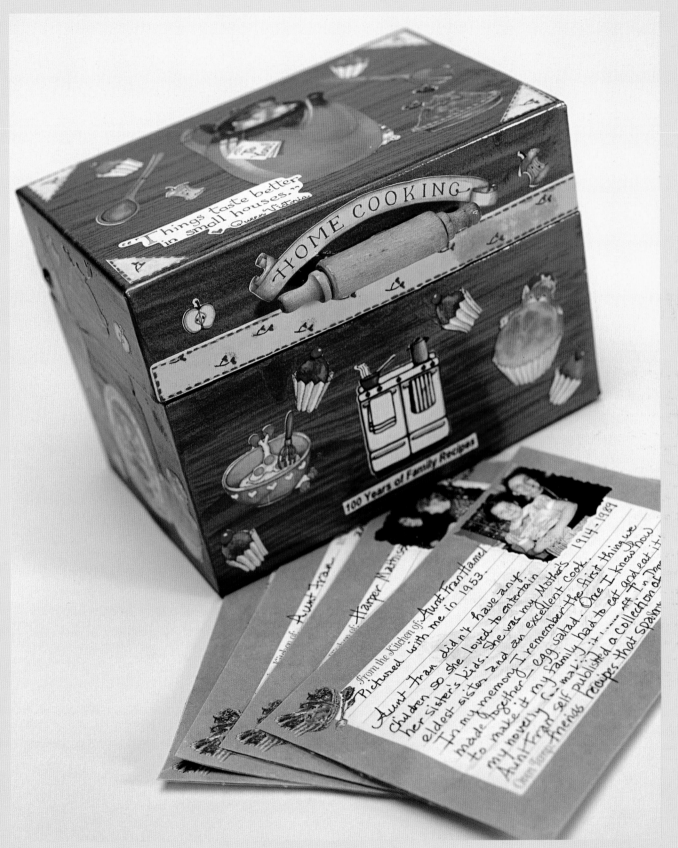

Design: Connie Sheerin

I created this clock using family pictures under glass nuggets so that every time I looked at the clock, I would remember my family. The same concept could take on many ideas and themes, like baby's first year, your favorite pet or pets, first-year anniversary pictures, and so on. The amber-colored glass nuggets give a slightly mellow look to the old black-and-white pictures of my mom's sisters. What a special little gift to give to anyone you love!

Family Photo Clock

MATERIALS

- 11" (28 cm) square wooden frame
- 8" (20 cm) tile with a hole for the clockworks
- 12 1½" (4 cm) diameter clear glass nuggets
- 12 color photocopies of photographs
- clock face rubber stamp
- *time* rubber stamp
- white textured paper
- metallic white pearl acrylic paint
- gold pigment stamp pad
- gold metallic paint
- high-gloss black spray paint
- archival glue
- Liquid Laminate
- black permanent ink stamp pad
- damp paper towel
- white craft glue
- set of black clockworks
- sawtooth picture hanger

1. Cover the wooden frame with two or three coats of high-gloss black spray paint until it is completely covered.

2. Tear the white paper into irregular pieces, about 2" (5 cm) square. Glue the paper pieces to the 8" (20 cm) tile with archival glue, overlapping the pieces to cover the front of the tile. Be sure to poke through the hole in the center (from the front side) before glue the dries.

3. Glue the color photocopies under the glass nuggets using Liquid Laminate. Push out any extra liquid with your finger, and wipe off the excess with a damp paper towel.

4. When the Liquid Laminate has completely dried, apply a coat of the metallic white pearl paint over the torn pieces of paper.

5. Stamp the word *time* all over the front of the tile. Stamp the clock face with the gold metallic paint, and glue it to the center of the front of the tile. Poke a hole though the center of the clock face to line up with the hole in the tile.

6. Use the archival glue to attach the picture nuggets around the outer edge of the tile to represent the hours on the clock.

7. After all the glue under the nuggets has dried, glue the tile into the wooden frame, and allow it to dry overnight.

8. Highlight the black frame using gold paint. You can either use your finger or a cosmetic sponge.

9. Attach the clockworks, following the directions on the package. Attach the sawtooth hanger to the middle of the upper back of the frame. You can now hang and enjoy your family clock.

Keepsake Tips

- Practice using the *time* stamp and permanent black ink on scrap paper before using it on the clock. Don't forget that this project is handmade—it doesn't have to be perfect to be just right.
- I found more pictures than I needed, so I added a magnetic strip to the back of the extra glass nuggets to adorn the refrigerator and the filing cabinets at work.

Design: Connie Sheerin

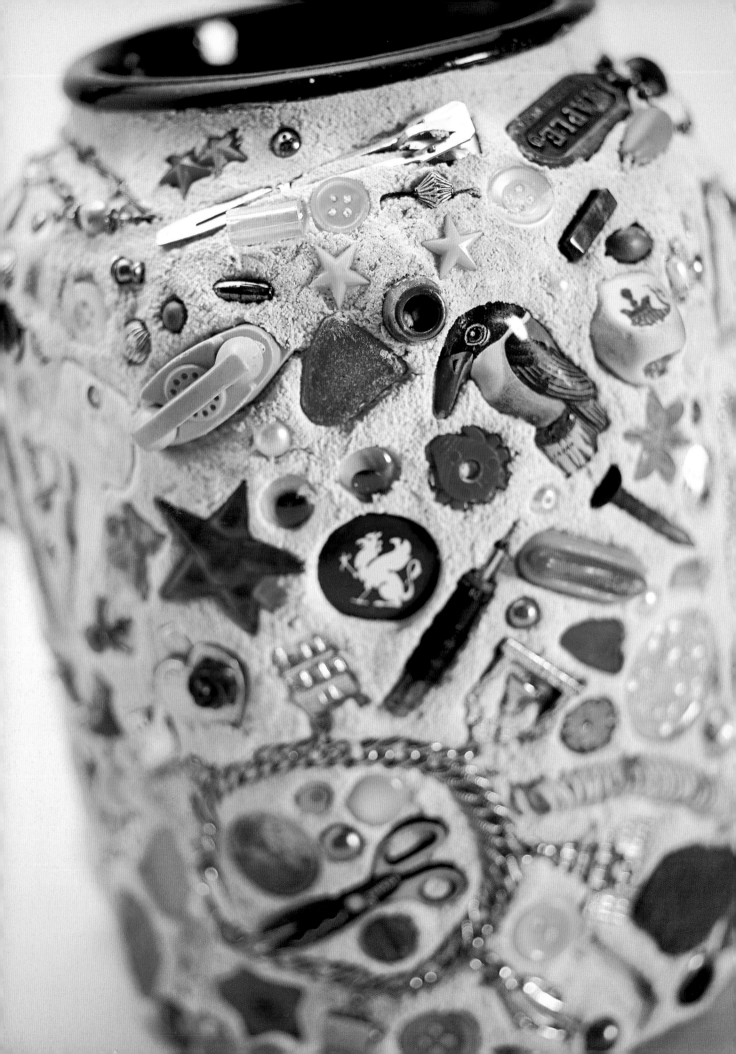

IN PRIMITIVE CULTURES, stories, proverbs, and cultural information were passed on orally from generation to generation. For example, the aboriginal people of Australia built their nomadic life around stories called songlines, which were told while walking and which served as maps, travelogues, and history lessons.

In Remembrance

In our high-tech culture, stories and information can be passed on with the click of a computer mouse. Crafters may be familiar with all the traditional crafting tools and techniques, but saving family treasures often presents the challenge of reproducing old, unique, and oftentimes fragile documents. To solve this problem, we used a combination of handcrafting techniques and modern technology, making computers, printers, and copy machines the new favorite tools to preserve history.

Cherished Memories

After losing someone close, it's sometimes difficult to face the items that have been left behind, but if done in the right spirit, you may find this experience rewarding and even therapeutic. Try to approach such a task as an opportunity to give these items a new life, one that will pay tribute to some very cherished memories. The projects in this chapter provide ideas for remembering some of those people who were dear to you. Each memory bears its own individual gift—another story told, another way to recapture our remembrances with both smiles and tears. Pulling those memories together in a creative way provides a special gift, one either to keep for yourself or to share with another person who has suffered this same loss. These physical symbols can be very powerful and immensely comforting as the grief subsides and the fond memories take its place.

A grandmother's button collection can become memory bracelets for all of her daughters and granddaughters. A few pieces of vintage costume jewelry can create a beautiful accent for a photo frame. A miscellaneous collection of small items can be transformed in a shrine, a collage, or a spirit jar. The simplest items, from handkerchiefs to kitchen utensils, can all be used as inspiration for your projects.

Sometimes it may seem as if there were years when nothing extraordinary happened—but just wait until you start really looking at and collecting the tidbits for these projects, and you will see that there was probably something worth remembering from every single day. There's a story behind every object. Take the time to share the stories and memorabilia of loved ones who have passed with the people in your life now. They will appreciate these tangible insights into your shared history.

A box of buttons can lead to a little journey through a lifetime. Special dresses, coats, baby clothes, and uniforms all come back to life when memories are triggered by these pieces of plastic and pearl. Our all-white version of this bracelet is made with pearls, mother-of-pearl buttons, and one glass shank button. This is a perfect way to turn a saved collection of buttons into special gifts for many members of a family.

Button Box Charm Bracelets

MATERIALS

· chain-link bracelet, either costume jewelry or sterling silver

· assorted vintage buttons (7 to 10 for each bracelet)

· 22-gauge wire

· beads or pearls (optional)

· wire cutter

· round-nose pliers

1. Cut a piece of wire 1½" (4 cm) long for each button you want to attach to the bracelet.

2. Using the wire-twisting diagram as a guide (see page 106), attach the buttons at even intervals along the bracelet.

3. Secure the wire by twisting it with the pliers, and cut off any extra wire with the wire cutters. Add beads or pearls, if desired.

Keepsake Tip

You can make different types of jewelry, such button "charms" hanging on a chain necklace (see the wire-twisting diagram at the back of the book) or by stringing shank buttons on a piece of elastic with the ends knotted.

Design: Janet Pensiero

I inherited a collection of kitchen utensils from my grandparents, and for years I've had them scattered around my kitchen. I wouldn't dream of throwing them out, but because the utensils really aren't functional, they needed to take a decorative place in my kitchen. This project works well for displaying kitchen utensils, but it would also work for other collections, such as tools, pot holders, mugs, or anything else that can hang. A small, tiered shelf or shadow box frame, painted and decorated with stories, is a great solution for displaying objects that can't be hung.

Family Collection Hanging Shelf

MATERIALS

- wooden shelf
- acrylic paint, two or three colors
- cup hooks
- color copies of photos
- printed out or handwritten family stories
- spray acrylic sealer
- white glue
- toy fork and spoon (optional)
- wire brads (optional)
- sandpaper
- damp cloth

1. Sand the shelf, and wipe it with a damp cloth to remove the dust. Paint the shelf with the base acrylic paint color of your choice. Apply a second coat if necessary.

2. Paint some areas of the shelf with the acrylic paint to coordinate with the objects you want to display. Apply a second coat if necessary. I attached toy wooden utensils to the front of the shelf with wire brads.

3. Write your stories out by hand, or print them out from your computer. Make sure the type is large enough—16- or 18-point type works well.

4. Glue your color copies of the photographs with your stories to the painted shelf using white glue, and let it dry.

5. After it is dry, spray the shelf with acrylic sealer. However, make sure you test the spray sealer with your computer printout before you spray the shelf. (If the ink on the printout runs, try a water-based polyurethane sealer). Screw in the cup hooks, and hang the items you want to display.

Grandmom Merlino used these kitchen tools in the basement kitchen, where she canned tomatoes.

Keepsake Tips

- Make the stories short and to the point. They are most effective if they can directly relate to something that is displayed nearby.

- This idea can be adapted to be used on a hanging shelf or even a bookcase. Dedicate each shelf to a different family member. Decoupage the inside back area with photos and stories.

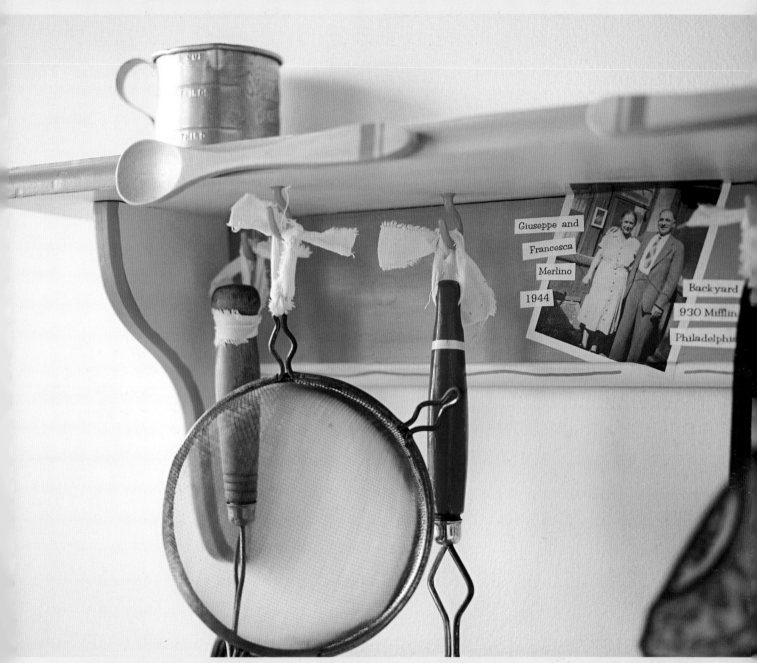

Giuseppe and
Francesca
Merlino
1944

Backyard
930 Mifflin
Philadelphia

Design: Janet Pensiero

At the American Visionary Art Museum in Baltimore, I saw some wonderful examples of folk art called spirit jars (also called memory jugs), which are containers that have been covered with putty or clay, and have various objects applied to cover their surfaces. These jars are believed to be a part of African-American burial customs, dating back to the time of slavery in this country, with the roots of the custom in African culture. Many cultures have similar rituals, which involve placing cherished objects with the body of the deceased or at the gravesite to ease the transition into the hereafter. These jars were also considered containers for the spirit of the departed and were used to celebrate a life. This twenty-first century spirit jar was made to celebrate a birthday, but other special events, like anniversaries or retirements, could also be celebrated with a jar like this.

Spirit Jar

MATERIALS

· ceramic jug, jar, or earthenware crock

· assorted items belonging to a person or persons to be remembered

· all-purpose, premixed stucco patch (such as DAP; see Keepsake Tip for more information)

· putty knife or flat plastic knife to spread stucco

· latex gloves (optional)

1. Use the putty knife to cover an area of the jug—about 6" (15 cm) square and about ¼" (6 mm) to ³⁄₈" (10 mm) thick—with stucco. The stucco starts to form a skin rather quickly, but takes a while to dry completely.

2. After a minute or two, press the small items into the stucco. Once the stucco has started to harden, you can press out any bumps or lumps with your fingers. Large or heavy items tend to slide down the sides, so keep the items small.

3. After you've covered the first area, let it dry for 30 minutes or so. Repeat this process until the entire jug is covered.

4. Any seams or cracks that appear can be patched with a tiny amount of stucco after it has begun to dry. A cotton swab works well for getting into the small spaces between the objects.

5. After the jug is completely covered, let it dry for several hours until the stucco hardens.

Keepsake Tip

DAP stucco patch works the best of all the materials I tested because it is sticky enough to hold the objects and can be touched up after it has dried. The stucco contains chemicals that may irritate the skin, so you may want to wear latex gloves while working with it.

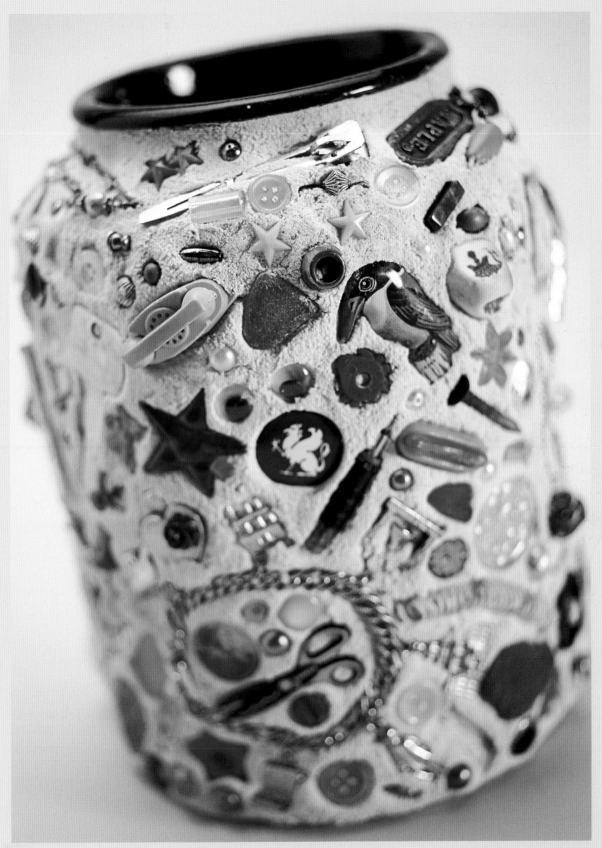

Design: Janet Pensiero

If your family photos are like mine, they're filled with aunts, cousins, and grandmothers wearing wonderful costume jewelry. It's great to inherit these baubles, especially when you know the ladies who enjoyed wearing them. Making the jewelry into a framed piece of art is a wonderful way to display it and appreciate it—and a terrific way to remember the former owners.

Costume Jewelry Art

MATERIALS

- picture frame
  (with the glass removed)
- ¼"-thick (12.7 mm) foam-core
- fabric or paper to cover the foamcore
- straight pins and sequin pins
- hot-glue gun and glue sticks
- costume jewelry
- craft knife
- straightedge

1. Use a craft knife and a straightedge to cut a piece of foamcore to fit inside the frame.

2. Choose a piece of fabric or paper to cover the foamcore.

3. Attach the jewelry using the hot-glue gun and pins. The hot glue can be used on anything with a flat back. Use a tiny amount of glue so that it doesn't show.

When attaching jewelry with pins, push in the pins at a slight angle so that the heads hold the piece to the board.

4. Don't forget to acknowledge the former owners on the side or back of the frame and include a photo if you have one.

GRANDMOM'S BROOCH

Design: Janet Pensiero

Sometimes the smallest items—an earring, an old cigar band, a token from an amusement park—can recall happy times with someone who's no longer around. My dad and I had a very special relationship. He was loving, kind, and always made me feel safe and special. I loved his great sense of humor and his sensitivity. At the same time, he was always ready to challenge me on what I thought was right and he thought was wrong. I gave my dad this small box when I was a little girl; now I use it to hold small mementos of him.

Dad's Memory Box

MATERIALS

- wooden box (any size)
- wood stain
- color photocopies of pictures of the person through the years
- archival glue
- Liquid Laminate
- decoupage scissors
- small paintbrush
- fine-line black felt-tip marker
- utility knife
- rubber stamps of words, like *love*, *laughter*, and *friend*
- stamp pad with permanent ink, any color
- self-adhesive cigar and cigar bands (optional)

1. The "Dad" box I had was perfect, but you can purchase any box and stain it with a wood stain of your choice.

2. Plan the arrangement of your color photocopies, and then trim them to your liking. Glue them to the box using the archival glue. Add any decorative touches, such as the self-adhesive cigars and cigar bands, that remind you of your special person.

3. Using the small paintbrush, coat the entire box with Liquid Laminate, and allow it to dry thoroughly.

4. When the laminate is completely dry, carefully trim any of the pictures that overlap the top and bottom of the box with a utility knife.

5. Randomly stamp words on the box that describe your person and your relationship to him or her. You can also add the dates of birth and death with the black felt-tip marker if you'd like.

Keepsake Tip

Glue a favorite picture to the underside of the box's lid for a special surprise. The picture I chose was the earliest one we had of my dad—at age four.

Design: Connie Sheerin

LOVE AND *FRIENDSHIP*, *FRIENDS* AND *LOVERS*—any way you say it, they are very special words in all of our vocabularies. The fun part about these two relationships is that, unlike our family relationships, we get to choose them. And often those relationships are as cherished and long-lasting as those with our families.

Love and Friendship

For many of us, our friends are just another type of family. The projects in this chapter range from beautiful and personal wedding keepsakes to fun and informal picture place cards for a dinner party. If your friends are like ours, then they will enjoy these gifts of the heart much more than any store-bought gift.

Special People

When you look through your collections of pictures of friends and lovers, you will surely find some that you have forgotten, but all will certainly bring a story to mind. Although some may have passed in and out of your life over the years, others may still be an important part of it. Many of these pictures and keepsakes can be made into wonderful gifts for those friends who still remain in your life—and you can treasure your memories together.

We have given you a variety of ideas, from the sublime to the fun, each creating a tactile memory of a moment in a shared friendship—from wedding celebrations to special dinners. Think of the gatherings you have with your friends as opportunities to document and preserve the time that you share with these special people in your life. Are you having a wedding shower? Why not invite all the guests to autograph the tablecloth with a special pen, and give the tablecloth to the bride at a later date? Are you hosting a potluck dinner party? Request that everyone send you the recipe from their dish, and begin to create a recipe book from all your parties.

In fact, turn your treasure keeping into a party—get friends together for a creative night called a "swap." Select a project or a theme, and have everyone make multiples, then exchange your creations at the end of the night. The biggest pleasure comes from seeing the individual expressions of the very same idea!

Ivy is traditionally used in bridal bouquets because of its symbolism. It stands for wedded love, fidelity, friendship, and affection. I've been to many weddings over the years—even caught the bouquet once—and I like to make this gift for special friends. Remember to pinch off two or three sprigs of ivy from the bouquet after the ceremony, and wrap them in a damp paper napkin until you get home. The new bride will be thrilled to have a living part of her bouquet come back to her, months after the flowers are gone.

Bridal Bouquet Ivy Pot

MATERIALS

- small terra-cotta flowerpot
- large glass pot or other glass container
- sheet moss
- white or pastel fine-line paint pen
- decorative ribbon or trim
- double-sided tape

1. Line the bottom of the glass pot with moss. Place the small terra-cotta pot centered on the moss. Make sure there is about $1/2$" (1 cm) of space between the sides of the small pot and the larger one.

2. Gently insert small pieces of moss in the space between the two pots until the cavity is completely filled.

3. With a white or pastel fine-line paint pen, write your message on the outside of the glass pot. You can also write your message for the outside of the pot on a small piece of paper, tape it to the inside of the glass pot, and trace the lettering with the paint pen.

4. Attach a piece of ribbon or trim to the top edge of the pot with double-sided tape.

5. Carefully transplant your rooted ivy into the terra-cotta pot

Keepsake Tip

Rooting ivy is simple. First remove two or three leaves from the cut end of the ivy sprigs. Place the cuttings in water with a small amount of plant food and allow them to sit for several weeks, making sure there is plenty of water, until roots begin to sprout. Then transfer the ivy to a small pot filled with potting soil. Water and feed the cutting until you present it to the bride.

This ivy was rooted from Kathy's bridal bouquet 9·27·97

Design: Janet Pensiero

It's so easy to create an iron-on photo transfer, and the possibilities for using this process are almost limitless. Type, artwork, and photographs can all be transformed into iron-ons with ease at most copy centers. All you need is an iron to complete the process. Most home computer printers are designed to use the iron-on transfer paper as well. Imagine a birth announcement turned into a sweet pillow for the baby's room. Or a real estate ad or flyer enlarged and presented to the new owners of the house as a special housewarming gift. This is a fun way to preserve newspaper clippings, too—the sportsman (or woman) in your house would love to have their winning game stats and photos immortalized on a pillow. And what about those album covers you can't bear to part with? Picture your easy chair filled with your favorite albums in pillow form!

Wedding Invitation Pillow

MATERIALS

- photo iron-on transfer of a wedding invitation
- small piece of solid colored fabric for iron-on
- coordinating fabric for front and back of pillow, approximately ½ yard (46 cm).
- polyester stuffing or pillow form
- trim
- pins
- needle and thread

1. Have an iron-on transfer made at your local copy center, or make one using your home computer. If you're using iron-on paper with your computer printer, be sure to follow package directions carefully. Iron the transfer to a solid piece of fabric, leaving a fabric border of 1" (3 cm) around the edge of the invitation.

2. Cut two pieces of fabric to the size you would like the finished pillow to be.

3. Center the fabric with the iron-on invitation on one piece of the pillow fabric and pin in place. Turn the edge over, and hand-stitch the invitation in place using a blind stitch. Sew or glue decorative trim around the edge of the invitation or in a random pattern.

4. Place the front sides together, and sew around three sides of the pillow shape. Then turn the pillow cover inside out, and fill it with polyester stuffing, or insert a pillow form. Hand-stitch the open side closed using a blind stitch.

Keepsake Tips

- Make a small pocket for the back of the pillow, and fill it with written remembrances of the happy couple.
- Many copy centers have special irons that work better than your home iron at transferring large iron-on images. They will usually iron them for you at no charge.

Kathleen Meyer & Timothy Peters

are getting married (to each other)
and we would like you to come to our wedding.

The ceremony will begin at 1:00 p.m. on September 27, 1997
at Corpus Christi Church, Charleston Road, Willingboro, New Jersey.

The reception will follow at St. Mary's Hall, Burlington, New Jersey.

Please respond by August 30, 1997.

Directions, map, and response card enclosed.

Please come!

Design: Janet Pensiero

Nothing takes you back to your younger and carefree days more than saved love letters, especially from someone still dear to you. When my mother showed me these letters she had saved from my dad, it made me realize how important handwritten letters are, as opposed to the electronic correspondence we use today. My dad's penmanship reminded me of his artistic, creative, and passionate way of expressing himself through writing, not to mention his great sense of humor.

Love Letters Envelope Wall Hanging

MATERIALS

· rusted metal envelope wall hanging, 7½" (19 cm)

· color photocopies of love letters

· color photocopies of the letter writer and recipient

· acid-free glue

· decoupage scissors

· decaled edge scissors

· lace

· fabric adhesive, such as Fabri-Tac

1. Make color photocopies of the letters, and cut out some of your favorite lines from the letters with the decaled scissors. You can use the decaled or decoupage scissors to cut out the pictures of the featured people.

2. Arrange your pictures and sentences until you like the design. You can trace the position of the pictures and sentences on a piece of paper for a template before actually gluing.

3. Glue some lace on the inside of the metal envelope with some fabric adhesive for a romantic touch.

4. Using the acid-free glue, apply each design, working from the background of your design to the foreground. Allow each layer to dry thoroughly before going to the next layer.

5. Add any additional touches to make the project personal and unique.

Keepsake Tip

Make color copies of both the letters and the envelopes so you can cut out special lines and the postage stamps and date to use as embellishment on the wall hanging.

Design: Connie Sheerin

We all save cards and small mementos from special occasions. But where do we put them?
Usually in a drawer with a rubber band around them. This project shows you how to create a
decorated keepsake box with your mementos, and you can even store any additional items inside
it. I hope this box will be a treasured memory for Karen and Brian, the bride and groom for
whom it was designed. Think about how many different occasions a box like this could be used
for, from a birth to a special birthday to an anniversary.

Wedding Keepsake Box

MATERIALS

- papier-mâché heart dome box, 10" x 10" x 5" (25 cm x 25 cm x 13 cm)
- one package of decorative tissue paper
- wedding invitation and save-the-date card
- one page of dried flowers and leaves
- tweezers
- 1' of gold trim
- decoupage medium, such as Mod Podge, in a satin finish
- white glue
- white acrylic paint
- two sponge brushes

1. Using a sponge brush, paint all parts of the box that will be visible with white acrylic paint.

2. Follow the directions that come with the box to assemble the top. Use white glue to attach the pieces together.

3. Cut the invitation to fit under the dome. Glue it in place with the white glue according to directions that come with box.

4. Use the tweezers to pick up the dried leaves and flowers. Dip each piece into the white glue, and place the pieces around the invitation to create a frame. Then glue the dome over the invitation. Measure and cut the gold trim, and glue it around the dome.

5. Tear the tissue paper into fairly large pieces, enough to cover the entire box, inside and out. Glue the pieces onto the box using the decoupage medium and a sponge brush.

6. Glue the save-the-date card and its envelope onto the bottom of the box. Apply a second coat of the decoupage medium.

Keepsake Tip

The save-the-date card's envelope tells the bride and groom whom the gift is from, and the postage stamp and postage mark add more documentation to the gift.

Design: Connie Sheerin

Dinners with family or friends, especially on special occasions, are always the best time for sharing and laughter. These place cards are a fun and memorable idea that are sure to evoke another story or memory. You could make these photo place cards on inexpensive napkin rings for favors to take home and start all over again with new ones for the next gathering.

Fun Photo Placecards

MATERIALS

· assortment of self-adhesive photo cards

· color photocopies of pictures that will fit nicely under the photo cards

· decoupage scissors

· dried flowers for embellishment (optional)

· inexpensive napkin rings

· epoxy glue, such as Glass, Metal & More

1. Trim the color photocopies to fit each photo card. Peel off the protective backing from the photo card, and attach the photocopy. Trim off any excess pieces of the picture.

2. Glue the photo cards onto the napkin rings with epoxy glue. Let dry and decorate with dried flowers, if desired.

3. Avoid writing on these—everyone needs to guess who is who and what the story is behind the pictures.

Keepsake Tip

The self-adhesive photo cards can be found in most craft and stationary stores. You can also use clear acetate cut to size. Attach the photo to the acetate with silver foil tape around the edges.

Design: Connie Sheerin

THAT FAMILIAR SAYING "when all is said and done" never seems to hold true for me. As soon as you think that you have things all wrapped up, the creative juices start to flow and you always come up with more ideas. We couldn't close the book without including a few of the pieces that created themselves along the way. It is our pleasure to offer you these projects, and if not for the deadline, they would

Gallery

extend for a hundred more pages. Just remember, these types of projects bring forth stories, love, treasures, and memories—there is no limit of where you will travel into your own gallery of treasures forever.

Family Linens Pillows

When you inherit the odds and ends of a linen closet, what do you do with all the mismatched pieces? Making them into pillows is a great way to display pieces that would normally be hidden in the linen chest. Two linen or damask napkins form the fronts and backs of these pillows. The crocheted pieces and buttons are sewn on by hand. Then a pillow form is inserted, and the open side is sewn shut. Don't limit yourself to napkins, either—you can use favorite old dresses, your grandmother's curtains, or even dish towels.

Design: Janet Pensiero

Vintage Chenille Baby Quilt

Old bedspreads, even if they're not handmade quilts, can trigger memories of childhood rooms or houses. If you have an old bedspread that is worn or stained, or even has a few holes, you can give it a new life in a baby's room as a quilt or a wall hanging. Cut a large piece of the bedspread—36" x 45" (91 cm x 114 cm) is the standard baby quilt size, but a 40" (102 cm) square works well, too. Cut a piece of coordinating fabric the same size and sew around three sides. Place a layer of quilt batting inside, and stitch up the open side. Tack the three layers together with embroidery floss every few inches or so. You can add vintage buttons or other bits of vintage crochet or embroidery. If there's a family story attached to the bedspread, you can write it on the back of the quilt with a permanent fabric marker. Then present the lucky baby with a little piece of family history.

Design: Janet Pensiero

Our House Guest Book

Memories of good times with visitors—family and friends alike—can be even more special in a personalized guest book. For the cover, enlarge a photo of your house on a black-and-white photocopier. Then, enlarge the enlargement to fit comfortably on your cover. Print the second enlargement onto four pieces of different colored paper—most copy centers have 11" x 17" (28 cm x 43 cm) paper in a range of colors. Cut the copies of the colored paper into quarters, making sure they align to create the original photo. Mount two pieces of cardstock together with double-sided mounting adhesive to make both the front and back covers. Then mount the quarter pictures onto the front cover, and cover them with plastic laminating film. Print out a title on your computer, or hand-letter it. For the inside of the book you can use any good quality paper, such as heavy-weight sketchbook paper. Bind the covers to the inside pages with the punch and ring binding system.

Keepsake Tip

Enlarging a photo twice on a photocopier creates the high contrast black-and-white photo effect used here. It's best to start with a lighter photograph to keep more detail in the photo.

Design: Janet Pensiero

Aunt Mary's Closet Evening Bag

Collecting the labels from favorite clothes is a great way to remember not only the clothes, but also the person who owned them. Aunt Mary's closet was an endless source of fascination for me as a kid, because she loved clothes and always had glamorous cocktail dresses for me to try on. I hand-stitched these labels onto a sandwich of two pieces of lightweight polyester-cotton fabric with a layer of polyester batting in between. To make a bag 7" (18 cm) square, cover an area roughly 7" x 14" (18 cm x 36 cm) with labels, and fold it in half. Blind stitching around the edge of each label creates the raised quilted effect. The handles are steel memory wire strung with vintage pearl beads. Use a vintage button and a loop of silk cord for the closure. For a simpler project, glue or stitch the labels onto a small purchased canvas bag.

Keepsake Tip

For a more elegant look, stitch pearls all around the edge of the bag.

Design: Janet Pensiero

License Plate Trip Journal

Two old license plates—cleaned, flattened out, and backed with felt—make the covers of this trip journal. After gluing a strip of folded flocked paper to the long edge of each license plate for the spine, back each plate with coordinating felt using iron-on fusible web. The inside of the book is up to you. You can use the versatile punch and ring binding system and fill it with blank pages for notes, maps, menus, or plastic sleeves for collecting mementos. For a finishing touch, glue two silver shank buttons in the holes of the license plates to simulate screw heads.

Keepsake Tips

- Wash and dry the license plates before you use them. It's important that they be as flat as possible, so straighten out any kinks and bumps as well.

- If you only have one license plate, use it for the front cover, and use a piece of mat board cut to size for the back cover.

Design: Janet Pensiero

Swimsuit Dress Form

This piece came about when I saw the dress form in my favorite rubber stamp store. I thought about the pictures of my grandparents in their old-fashioned bathing suits—and, compared to today's bathing suits, about how hot my grandparents must have been. It's amazing how quickly fashion became more comfortable in less than 20 years. Add some images of seashore-related items, like fish and seashells, among the pictures, and embellish the form with some seashore charms.

Keepsake Tip

The dress form shapes have become very popular for home decorating pieces. You can choose any clothing theme, such as the '70s or prom night.

Design: Connie Sheerin

Translucent Envelope Book

You can purchase large plastic document envelopes in a range of colors at office supply stores. By binding several envelopes together with large rings, you can create a childhood souvenir book in which to keep special things like tiny socks and T-shirts, finger paintings, and report cards.

Design: Janet Pensiero

Decoupaged Makeup Case

I have always loved this little makeup case. It belonged to my Aunt Fran, but you can find one in second-hand stores and at garage sales. I really enjoyed choosing some paint to give it new life. Then I decoupaged it with cosmetic-themed prints. For a finishing touch, I used a rubber stamp and some polymer clay to make a nameplate. The case houses my scarves and goes with me on special road trips. It's perfect when I want just a little more attention—which it certainly does attract!

Keepsake Tip

You can also collect paper items from trips and decoupage a memory suitcase as a decorative piece.

Design: Connie Sheerin

Aunt Rose's Handkerchief Sachets

I used my Aunt Rose' handkerchiefs for this project, but you can use your grandmother's monogrammed linen napkins or a piece from your mother's old kitchen curtains to create a beautiful and aromatic sachet. Wash and iron the handkerchief, then lay it flat, right side down, with the four corners making a diamond shape. Using the diagram on page 107 as a guide, fold the left and right sides to the center, overlapping the points to achieve the desired width. Fold the bottom point up and under. Hand-stitch along the left and right edges of the folded handkerchief. Fold a piece of polyester batting in half to create a pocket that will hold the potpourri inside the handkerchief envelope. Insert the batting pocket into the folded handkerchief, and fill with potpourri or scented dried botanicals. Fold the top flap over and secure it with buttons or beads.

Keepsake Tip

You can also place a small amount of potpourri in the center of a square handkerchief, pull the four corners up, and tie it with a ribbon for a simple sachet.

Design: Janet Pensiero

Patterns

GRANDFATHER'S TIE PILLOW

pages 32-33

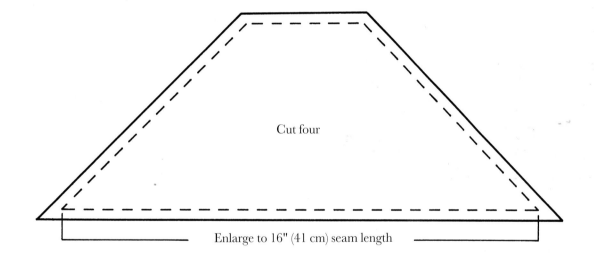

Cut four

Enlarge to 16" (41 cm) seam length

Patterns

BUTTON BOX CHARM BRACELETS

pages 60-61

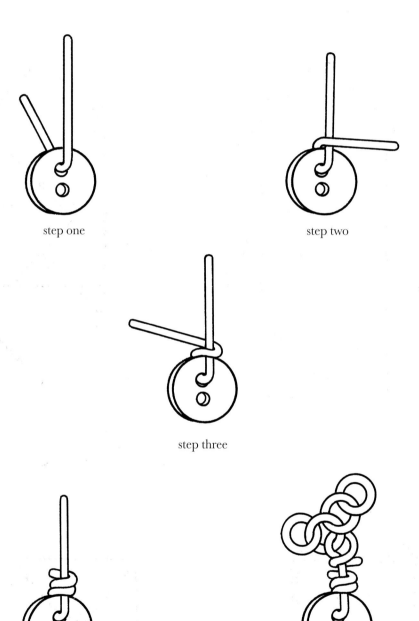

step one

step two

step three

step four

step five

AUNT ROSE'S HANDKERCHIEF SACHETS

pages 102-103

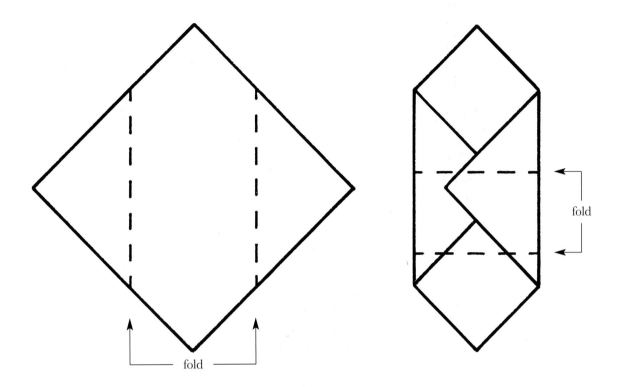

fold

fold

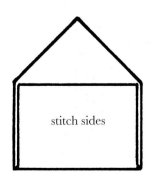

stitch sides

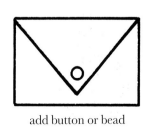

add button or bead

Resources

ADHESIVE PRODUCTS

Beacon Adhesives
125 S. MacQuesten Pkwy.
Mount Vernon, NY 10550
www.beaconcreates.com

COLOR COPIES AND TRANSFERS

Kinko's
Stores throughout U.S.
www.kinkos.com

CRAFT PENS

Chartpak
One River Rd.
Leeds, MA 01053
www.chartpak.com

CUTTING TOOLS

Fiskars, Inc.
7811 W. Stewart Ave.
Wausau, WI 54401
1-800-950-0203
www.fiskars.com

DOUBLE-SIDED ADHESIVE TAPE

Grafix
19499 Miles Roads
Cleveland, OH 44128
1-800-447-2349

DRIED FLOWERS

Nature's Pressed
P.O. Box 212
Orem, UT 84059
1-800-850-2499
www.naturespressed.com

Hanko Designs
875-A Island Dr. #286
Alameda, CA 94502
www.hankodesigns.com

FABRIC PAINT AND ADHESIVES

DecoArt
P.O. Box 386
Stanford, KY 40484
1-606-365-3193
www.decoart.com

GENERAL CRAFT SUPPLIES

Connie Sheerin Enterprises
P.O. Box 246
Lansdowne, PA 19050
www.mosaicmania.com
Concraft@aol.com

Crafts ala Cart
1612 Union Valley Rd.
West Milford, NJ 07480
www.craftsalacart.com

DC&C
Decorator & Craft Corporation
Rusty tin-tiques & papier-mâché
428 S. Zelta
Wichita, KS 67207
1-800-835-3013

Delta Crafts
www.deltacrafts.com
1-800-423-4135

HobbyCraft
Stores throughout UK
Head Office: Bournemouth
01202 596100

John Lewis
Stores throughout UK
Head Office: Oxford St.
London, W1A 1EX
020 7269 7711

Plaid Enterprises, Inc
P.O. Box 7600
Norcross, GA 30091-7600
www.plaidonline.com

Ranger Industries
15 Park Rd.
Tinton Falls, NJ 07724
www.rangerink.com

GLASS
Sigma Glass Co.
149 Garrett Rd.
Upper Darby, PA 19082
1-610-352-3998

HANDMADE PAPER
Loose Ends
P.O. Box 20310
Keizer, OR 97307
www.looseends.com

PAINTBRUSHES
Loew-Cornell
563 Chestnut Ave.
Teaneck, NJ 07666-2490
www.loew-cornell.com

POLYMER CLAY
Kato Polyclay
Donna Kato, The Art of Polymer Clay
www.donnakato.com
www.prairiecraft.com

PUNCH AND RING BINDING SYSTEM
Rollabind Inc.
3117 N.W. 25th Ave.
Pompano Beach, FL 33069
1-800-438-3542
www.rollabind.com

RUBBER STAMPS, INK,
AND EMBOSSING SUPPLIES
Inkadinkado
Woburn, MA 01801
www.inkadinkado.com

Create an Impression
A Rubber Stamp Store and so Much More!
56 E. Lancaster Ave.
Ardmore, PA 19003
1-610-645-6500

UNFINISHED WOOD PRODUCTS
Walnut Hollow Farm, Inc.
1409 State Rd. 23
Dodgeville, WI 53533
www.walnuthollow.com

GENEALOGY WEB SITES
www.ellisislandrecords.com
www.genealogy.com
www.afrigeneas.com
www.ancestry.com

IF YOU'RE ON THE EAST COAST OF THE
U.S., WE'D RECOMMEND A VISIT TO
The American Visionary Art Museum
800 Key Highway
Baltimore, MD 21230
1-410-244-1900

Acknowledgments

Many thanks to my extraordinarily talented co-author and partner in creativity, Janet Pensiero. Her ideas are always amazingly unusual and appeal to my creative appreciation. I say this also in the hope that she will continue to make me more friendship memories, like the white button bracelet in this book. When she made me this bracelet, I knew that I wanted her to be my co-author on this book. I don't share the patience required for some of her undertakings, but then I sew everything with a bottle of fabric glue! I am sure that's why we have such a great appreciation for each other's talents.

My thanks to my patient and persistent editor at Rockport Publishers, Mary Ann Hall. I have worked with Mary Ann before, but now I've had the opportunity to tie her up yet again with a project of larger proportions.

Kudos to Pamela Hunt, who has the patience and tolerance of a saint to put this book together in a way that makes sense to me but also provides enjoyment for all of you.

Lastly I want to thank my friends and loves, and my family, who were a great part of this book, and my Angel the Dog, my teacup terrier, who is sleeping at my feet, dreaming of bones—her treasures forever. And last, but never least, my good husband, Ken Williams, who eats lots of take-out, never complains about crafts "everywhere," and stands behind me in all I do.

Connie Sheerin
September 2001

First, I must thank my friend and colleague Connie Sheerin. She had the terrific concept for this book and was kind enough to share it with me by asking me to join her as co-author. Connie puts creativity into everything she does, and her generosity of spirit touches everyone she knows.

I am grateful for the support of my creative friends during the process of putting this book together, especially Nancy Hotchkiss, who made a last-minute run to the museum for spirit jar information.

Thanks also to the gang at Rollabind, for the supplies and support, and Pamela Hunt, for helping me organize words and eliminate run-on sentences.

I'd also like to thank my family: my sister and brother-in-law, Frances and Jan Carr, who gathered up family papers; my nephew Matt, who contributed his writing; my niece Katie, who contributed her artwork; Aunt Mary Merlino, who inspired an evening bag; and my late grandparents, whose stories I will continue to keep.

Finally, I'd like to thank my parents, Ben and Angie Pensiero, who have always supported and promoted my creative efforts, and always made sure I had enough crayons and blank paper.

Janet Pensiero
September 2001

About the Authors

Connie Sheerin is a designer, author, and TV personality with 30 years of experience. Connie has been a guest demonstrator on numerous television shows, including *The Rosie O'Donnell Show*, *The Carol Duvall Show*, *Home Matters*, *Handmade by Design*, and *Willard Scott's Farm & Garden Journal*. She is CEO and president of Crafts ala Cart™, a business based on teaching crafts to others. She is also a contributor to many crafts magazines and is the author of three other books. She resides in Lansdowne, Pennsylvania. Visit Connie Sheerin's Web sites at www.craftsalacart.com or www.conniesheerin.com.

Janet Pensiero is an award-winning designer with more than 20 years of experience as an art director, toy designer, and craft artist. Since graduating from Moore College of Art and Design, in Philadelphia, she has designed everything from ads to a sign system for the Philadelphia Zoo to activity toys for children. Most recently, she was Senior Project Designer and Art Director at Craftopia.com. Her varied background and wide range of experience provide an unlimited source of inspiration for the craft projects she designs and executes. Her work has been featured in several magazines and books, including *Hand Lettering for Crafts* (Rockport Publishers). She lives in Philadelphia, Pennsylvania.